TEARS OF ROSE WATER

by Maya Serbu

Tears of Rose Water

Tears of Rose Water

ISBN: 978-1-988215-72-3

Layout and Design
One Thousand Trees
www.onethousandtrees.com

*This book is dedicated
to **Dave Nagle**, without whom it would
have never been written. Thank you for
showing me how powerful a curious mind
can be, for pushing me to pursue my
dreams and continuing to inspire me
every single day.
To my **Mother**, who taught me what it
means to be independent.
To my **Father**, who taught me
the meaning of resilience.
To **Patricia**, who reminds me every day
there's a new reason to smile.
To **Mike**, who reminds me that
practice makes perfect.
To my **Friends**, who show me that
love truly has no judgement.
To the **People** who told me my dreams
were impractical, thank you for giving
me that much more of a reason
to prove you wrong.
And to **Me**, for never giving up on
myself, this is my heart & soul.
I love you.*

Tears of Rose Water

Maya Serbu

Acknowledgements

I have to start by thanking my 9th grade English teacher Mr. Nagle. I remember his response the first time he read my work was simply: "Writing is your jam, isn't it?" From that moment on he has supported me, reading every poem I brought to his judgmental face. I still live by what you told me once, "Publishing the book is not the joy, becoming a famous author isn't the joy. Happiness for you is the writing itself." Thank you Nagle, I did it.

I have to thank my former guidance counsellor, Ms. Greer, for all the encouragement she gave me to use writing as a creative outlet and for doing all she could to help me navigate the stormy days you will read about in the pages to come. Thank you for believing I was strong enough to take on the world when I couldn't believe for myself.

Another huge thank you to my publisher Lisa Browning. Thank you for taking a chance on a teenager from a small town with a passion for poetry. Thank you for believing I was good enough. You've made my dreams a reality and I am eternally grateful.

Lastly, thank you to my friends, the best ones I'll ever have, the ones who make every day a little lighter. Thank you for making me feel like I matter, for giving me purpose, and for your constant support in all that I do. I love you guys forever.

Maya Serbu

As she stood there
rose water rolled down her cheeks
it collected under her chin for a moment
before dripping into the pavement
it was in that moment she realized
the only flowers we ever seem to pick
are the ones with thorns
-tears of rose water

Tears of Rose Water

Maya Serbu

Storm clouds

*

The sunlight

*

& The seeds

Tears of Rose Water

Prologue

This book is a collection of moments, feelings and people captured in time. Some are inspired by real events, some are little whispers of make believe, but all mean something to me. It is organized by the sad parts of life, the things that make it good again, and the people & things that stick around, no matter the weather. Read these pages how they were written, without afterthought. Allow yourself to simply feel and be. Thank you.

Tears of Rose Water

Maya Serbu

Storm clouds

Tears of Rose Water

don't worry my darling,
i no longer long for you the way i did
all those years ago
i am simply aching for the person you
used to be
-the you i knew

"please don't go," he begged "i love
you."
"you don't love me," she whispered.
"you just love the idea of me."

that day she watched him walk away
down the sidewalk where they first met
and she stood under the streetlight for
a moment thinking about how hard it
would be to forget his smell
-**goodbye**

that night she sat on the phone with him
for hours
cradling the receiver
they didn't need to speak
she just listened to him cry for awhile
because sometimes pain needs to be felt.
without it, we'd forget what it means to
be happy

Maya Serbu

she woke up every morning with sleep in
her eyes
surrounded by an air of melancholy

that night she walked aimlessly around
her empty house
barefoot
wearing his shirt
her face stained with tears and mascara
and as the clock turned to 12:00am
she knew
he wasn't coming back
-*when he left*

Maya Serbu

she saw cities in his green eyes
but he's seen green eyes in every city
-she was meaningless

Tears of Rose Water

i am completely enamoured of you my
darling
since i first saw you
i still don't know why i picked you
but those butterflies will forever be
carved into my heart

that moment she knew she had to save
herself
no one else was going to revive her
she had buried herself alive in her own
doubt
she needs to dig herself out before she
suffocates
-it was 4am

"we should be daydreaming about life
after high school, not hoping we survive
till then," she whispered, choking back
tears
trying to steady her breath
-**high school isn't like the movies**

Maya Serbu

"this is the kind of shit i don't need
i cannot afford to sink back down to
that dark place again-
-it's the kind of place you only escape
once,
and that's if you're lucky."
she mentally screamed at him as she
watched him sit on the couch
-oblivious

even though he knows you're no longer
his, sometimes all he can think about
are the 'what ifs' and 'maybes'
and the love that could be hidden
in the shadows of meant to be
-***broken hope***

Maya Serbu

no need to wipe my tears away darling
no one seems to notice the mascara
flooding down my cheeks like they used
to

brown eyes
careful with those
they'll get you every time

despite how torturous it was to see him
hurting so immensely
she grinned at him, tousled his hair and
they laughed for a moment
"i love you," she reminded him as she
watched him walk back up the sidewalk
he looked back at her and paused for a
moment before smiling back at her and
calling out
"i love you too"

we grow up thinking monsters are only
under our beds with green fur and sharp
teeth
however, the real monsters look just
like ordinary people
and the ones with sparkly eyes,
those are the ones to watch out for

Maya Serbu

as kids we are taught that skunk is only
smelt on highways during long car rides
but as we grow up our innocence begins
to slowly die
when we smell skunk on every street
corner, burning between someone's
fingertips
-*"drugs" used to be advil*

"i don't need you to say anything,
i just need you to let me miss it.
because sometimes in the middle of the
night,
our lost love appears like fireflies."

"i'm just not gonna care about him
anymore." she said with such finality
and determination set in her chestnut
eyes, i didn't have the heart to tell
her that it would be impossible to
forget the butterflies he set loose in
her stomach and how he made her feel in
a way no one else ever had before
-12:43am

Tears of Rose Water

and then you called me princess and i
knew i was fucked

i have always seen the world with rose
coloured glasses
In a world of social media and small
talk i still have faith in finding the
love of my life and having real
conversations
i want to know people, down to their
core but everyone's minds are becoming
shallow, very few people are capable of
having a deep conversation
language is being killed by the very
people who created it
the worst part about all of this is i am
still wearing these rose coloured
glasses
i still believe that we can salvage what
is left of humanity
and it is the few old souls left in this
world that need to save people from
themselves
before it's too late
-reconcile

Tears of Rose Water

there's bad in everything good
even water kills flowers
-*revelations*

i really thought you cared, that deep
down you had gold hidden behind your
tough exterior
i thought your pretty eyes and innocent
smile made you genuine
but no
your reputation always comes first
behind closed doors you are sweet and
honest
but you made a promise you could not
keep
i will forever wonder what it would feel
like to have you truly care
but you never did
so i never will

those afraid of dying are equally afraid
of living
-reality check

Maya Serbu

i fear i've just taught someone how to
stop loving me
-**a scary short story**

"but i want him, that's the problem.
even though he hurt me my heart thinks i
still need him. and even worse, my brain
is starting to believe it."
-*addiction*

Maya Serbu

no one cares about leaves until they're
dead on the ground in pretty colours.
remember that.
-invisible suffering

Tears of Rose Water

at the end of each day her flower died
and her soul became rotten throughout
the night,
bitter and forgetful of all the beauty
it once held
-3am demons

i know it hurts
but your sunflower garden must be weeded
of toxicity and watered with tears
before it can blossom
-*self care*

Tears of Rose Water

trace your fingers down the mascara
stains of my tears
they are like a map leading to where i
hurt
if you follow them down my cheeks
they continue along my neck
past my collarbones
always leading back to a new break in my
heart
-the beauty in the hurt

Maya Serbu

mistakes are simply memories riddled
with regret

Tears of Rose Water

i wait in agony for the day life will
finally be what we used to talk about
when we were kids, when our hearts were
pure, our intentions were innocent, our
eyes full of promise
naive, simple, curious
the days we believed nothing came after
"happily ever after."
when we believed in fairytales,
spontaneous kisses in the rain and
crepes on sunday mornings
when "i love you" meant forever and
promises couldn't be broken.
now i wait in agony for my own kids to
grow up with the same unrealistic ideas
carved into their hearts and painted
across their eyes
-broken world

the ignorant men in the shadows always
seem to outshine the rest
the loud arrogant abusers are the ones
that seem to control society
their opinions are the ones no one seems
to ask for
but are somehow always heard
-*unfair*

i know there's more to our story
i just don't know how long until you
come back into the book
So i'll dog ear our moments and
patiently hope
-***bookmarked***

i crave reassurance
i ache to hear "you're not ok and that's
ok"
i long for someone to explore the
emotions hidden in my tired eyes
i want somebody to notice when i'm
distant and low
i want to be held and spoken to softly
i want to be told I'm not alone
i want love
the problem is, your love speaks a
different language
-what i need

"your eyes aren't lighting up"
i panicked, faking a smile desperate to
make them light the way they used to
but
your eyes only light up with pure
honesty
genuinely
willingly
you have to find something real
stop faking
you aren't hopeless
just a little burnt out
-*light switch*

Maya Serbu

it is only in the late hours of the
night
that i let myself wander deep into the
corners of my mind

"i'm sorry" she sniffled, tears welling
in her eyes
"for what?" her reflection asked.
"for hating the only person that's been
there all my life, no matter what."
-*Self Love is hard*

she walked alone that night
under the stars
thinking
hoping
desperately searching for a reason to
not lie down in the street and sleep
forever
-lost

"she's the most beautiful girl I've ever
seen," he said to her.
and she smiled despite everything,
because she remembered when she was once
that girl to him too
-*bittersweet*

they punish me when i lash out
but they have no idea how long i've kept
my words hidden behind my zippered lips
and grinding teeth
-silenced

Tears of Rose Water

if only people changed as easily as
trees in autumn,
from green to golden
on the highway in the middle of nowhere
it could save us from a lot of pain
-sometimes people can't change

"when do you want to lose your
virginity?" he asked hungrily
"when i'm in love with someone who's in
love with me."
i whispered breathlessly

Tears of Rose Water

you say you want me but when? when i'm
crying in the middle of the night and
need a hug? when i decide to go for a
drive just to listen to the radio? when
i look up at you with tired eyes and
stress carved into my face? when i want
to go dance under the rain in the middle
of summer? or do you just want me in bed
or at a party or painted across your
phone screen for all of your friends to
judge and rate? and what's going to
happen if they disapprove? will you drop
me for something better and pretend i
was never an option? did you mean it
when you said you wanted me? did leaving
break you as much as it shattered me?
were you too afraid to love me?
do you ever think about me? do you ever
wake up in the middle of the night and
wonder if i'm crying? do you ever wish i
was there to sing along to the radio
when you're driving? do you ever think
about how beautiful i am without makeup
even when my eyes have dark circles and
my face is worn out from stress? do you
ever look out your window when it's
raining and wish you saw me dancing in
the street? you wanted me for all the
wrong reasons and the worst part about
it is, that i still want you
-questions i'm too afraid to ask

46

wanna know a secret?
i'm desperately in love with you and my
heart is broken into little pieces
because you don't even know my name
-you will never read this

Tears of Rose Water

and somehow
you won the game when you promised you
weren't playing
-*cheat*

the moon and sun had never met
but every morning the moon died so that
the sun could wake
-*sacrifice*

Tears of Rose Water

"you are quite the enigma, my darling."
he spoke softly, his eyes wandering with
curiosity
"oh love," she giggled at him
"the mystery is half the fun," she
replied, batting her eyelashes at him
before walking away
leaving him hungry

and in your hands i put my heart
-*mistakes*

no matter what you said
no matter how sweet it sounded
your words were only made of moonlight
and your whispers
full of stars
-your love was make believe

Maya Serbu

he was kind to her in those last
fleeting moments of marriage,
perhaps so they could remember each
other the way they used to
-*divorce*

there's something quite chilling about
freshly fallen snow
it lay silent
eerie
perfect
one of mother nature's nightmares

that night she held him as he cried
he walked her home and they talked for
hours under the streetlight as the quiet
snow fell around them
they hugged goodbye and walked different
ways
both fighting tears as they looked back
at each other wistfully
-*"don't leave"*

Tears of Rose Water

it had been months since she thought of
him
but that morning she smelled coffee
and she remembered how sweet his lips
tasted after breakfast
-*trigger*

Maya Serbu

she had spent her whole life plucking
petals off of sunflowers
chanting "he loves me, he loves me not"
she had no idea that all along
he was allergic to the pollen

57

Tears of Rose Water

Maya Serbu

The sunlight

Tears of Rose Water

he had never met someone so good
she was filled with it
it was as if she was made up of sunlight
-*purity*

Tears of Rose Water

surround yourself with people who make
your heart smile and your soul golden

so they danced and laughed in the middle
of the street, and forgot what it meant
to be sad for a little while
-happiness doesn't need rhythm

Tears of Rose Water

in the morning the golden sun would
always make her hazel eyes glow
like melted honey with drops of emerald
the corners of her eyes would crinkle
and her dimples would form like little
puddles in her cheeks
every time she smiled that damn smile
-**beautiful**

it is a beautiful thing to know someone
so intensely
to have tasted their laughter in the air
to have let their tears stain your skin
to have blown eyelashes from their
cheeks
and to have put your heart in someone
else's hands and trust them not to break
it
that is the definition of beauty
-***trust***

she drove down the highway
gazing at the horizon painted in red,
orange and yellow
daydreaming
with crystals in her eyes
-driving home from work

you deserve a love that always feels
like summer
-*easy romance*

"i think he may still be a little in
love with you."
"i think that's okay," she whispered.

Maya Serbu

she watched the leaves change colours
one evening
in awe and envy of their beauty
so the next morning
she lay on the ground
and buried herself in the golden sea

i crave to travel, i long to explore
to plant a little bit of myself in every
new ground i walk on
to leave a trail of light everywhere i
go
to be utterly spontaneous
and simply miraculous
-*discover*

some moments are like snowflakes
most beautiful when left untouched
-cherish, don't change

it had been almost 3 months since they
had last spoke
but when he called her that night it was
as if no time had passed
they laughed and teased each other as if
it was only yesterday
and she finally felt ok again
-magic at 8pm on a wednesday

Maya Serbu

i knew i was in trouble when i thought
everything you ever said to me sounded
like a love letter
- *falling*

Tears of Rose Water

i miss you in the mornings
when we used to talk and laugh in bed
when the warm sun shone through the
curtains, mixing with the cool october
breeze that was slipping in through a
crack in the window
when we would lay together for hours
falling in and out of sleep to the
sounds of the quiet neighbourhood and
the smell of the crisp autumn air
filling the house
when i felt content, like we were the
only people alive and we could just
simply live

the safest place i think you could ever
be is in someone's arms,
your head on their chest,
listening to their heartbeat
-*two can become one*

you called me beautiful
you told me you loved my smile
and just like that
i fell
-at *first sight*

there will always be the one that feels
different
the butterflies seem more vigorous
the smile comes easier
the heart beats quicker
and it feels right
-*i hope you find this*

that day he was walking home and he ran
into her
it was the first time they'd talked in
years
they were basically strangers
they made small talk before parting ways
down different paths
and she stood there for a minute
watching him walk away
and that was truly the first moment she
thought,
"maybe i could love him"
-*the moments he doesn't remember*

they looked at each other with so much
love in their eyes,
their smiles riddled with desire
-need

they looked up at the dark sky as the
stars spilled across it.
as they watched the indigo canvas become
dusted in glitter,
their breaths turned to fog and drifted
into the darkness
-nights to remember

meeting you, my love
was pure serendipity

that morning she rolled over into a
puddle of sunlight
she sat up and yawned as it warmed her
despite the chill the december air held
the sun was still beautiful
and so was she
-why i love sundays

"you're beautiful," he whispered as the
wind took his words with it into the
dark night
but not before she heard it
he watched her smile as she looked down
at the ground
and he stood there
staring at her
staring at him
as if for the very first time
-love reclaimed

Tears of Rose Water

his smile is the kind that makes you
forget that roses have thorns

after she met him
she became numb to all things bitter
because of the sweetness she heard in
his voice
-hypnotized

you always seem to be there to patch my
broken heart with reassurance,
to dry my eyes of sorrow,
to make me laugh when the sky is
falling,
and to steady my mind
when the earth is shaking
-*loyalty*

she walked down the street with her eyes
full of stars and wildflowers growing
out of her ears
-*she lived as if she were art*

yes we were kids
young, dumb and innocent
but we snuck out to look at the stars
we kissed in front of the blushing moon
and we felt happy for once
-*bliss*

Maya Serbu

as she lay in the grass
watching the dim stars grow brighter and
the indigo sky become darker
breathing in the cool september night
air
she felt truly,
amicable

we laid on my kitchen floor laughing at
1am tipsy off a couple beers we stole
and i could see us 10 years from now
drunk off too much red wine telling and
retelling our dumb stories of
adolescence and it made me have faith
that not all good things have to come to
an end
-best friends

Maya Serbu

the only oceans she every truly adored
were the ones in his eyes,
which seemed to go on forever

as i sat there nursing my cup of coffee
i felt my eyes begin to light up the way
they once did
the sun hung low as it began its lift
into the summer sky as it did every
morning and i let myself exhale
everything felt good
i felt happy again
-light switch pt.2

no matter who comes into my life
no matter how vigorously they sweep me
off my feet
a part of my heart will always belong to
you my darling
and a part of yours, to me
-*dear first love*

it was beautiful
the way the golden leaves fell to the
ground as the sun made the morning dew
shimmer
and the way nothing seemed to matter in
that instant
-*look around you*

we take so many little moments for
granted
like sunsets and routine "i love you's"
we must learn to cherish them
otherwise we won't realize when they are
our lasts
-remind your people

i am finally rebuilding the house in my
ribcage where the butterflies lived
-when he came home

Maya Serbu

she watched the sun rays peek between
the tree branches
and in that moment she realized mornings
are the most beautiful things
-***beginnings***

Tears of Rose Water

i never liked school
you were my favourite subject,
i was always studying your eyes
wondering how they always seemed to
sparkle
-now i'm failing history

that night after she left he leaned
against the doorway
still tasting her lips on his
and he wondered if it was really meant
to be her in the end
-***perhaps***

Tears of Rose Water

i can't wait to marry my best friend
to dance in the living room on a tuesday
afternoon
to try to quietly giggle after the kids
are in bed
to drink red wine and watch
documentaries on friday nights
to be utterly and perfectly
in love
-love lightens life

sunday mornings are my favourite part of
the weekend
the way the sun leaks through the blinds
and the golden warmth consumes the bed
waking up after the wild saturday night
before with your best friends
sharing smiles and silent laughs as you
slowly come to life again, untangling
your legs from the clean white bed
sheets
walking down the hall in bare feet and
baggy t shirts to the kitchen
sunday means lazy
sunday means leaving the kitchen
cabinets dusted with flour and the
counters sticky with syrup
sunday is a reminder to be carefree once
in a while
because without sunday mornings
adulthood will devour us
-*savour*

Tears of Rose Water

"what's home to you?" i asked him under
the indigo night
he looked at me with stars dusted across
his eyes as lust dangled from his lips
the dull streetlight formed his shadow
across the sidewalk as he leaned in and
whispered
"you"

Maya Serbu

i sat up in bed that morning
wrapped in my covers
i watched the dust dance under the
sunlight for a moment
as the birds and butterflies giggled
outside my window
-*good morning*

that morning the air smelled of wet
pavement and chimney smoke
all the trees were bare
quiet snowflakes began tangling
themselves into her hair for a moment
before melting away into nothingness
-*winter*

she saw how beautiful the wild daisies
were
so she spent days chewing on their
petals
waiting for the bees and hummingbirds to
flock her
-**mother nature's daughter**

the people who are like sunlight
embodied,
those are the people i will spend my
days with.

Maya Serbu

"second chances are not weak, they are
human and filled to the brim with hope."
-forgiveness

"you okay?"
"just remembering," she smiled.

& The seeds

Tears of Rose Water

if people were truly meant to be alone
God wouldn't have made more

so God,
please be good to my best friends
for i couldn't bear to see the lights of
my life grow dim
-**thank you**

it is rare to know someone who has so
much in common with you
who has lived through all your traumas
who has stuck by when things were hard
it is rarer though, when that person is
your family
your blood
your history
your childhood
which is not something everyone gets the
privilege of having
-for Abi

that night she sat in her bedroom
humming
painting herself in colours
and as she sat there
dusted in glitter
her passion was born
-Rachel the beauty school dropout

Maya Serbu

the simplest things brought her joy
watching tv
eating takeout
listening to him sing
and drum on the steering wheel on the
drive to the grocery store
her world became brighter
and he fell madly in love with her
-when she met him

as we shared a laugh
spoke about pain we've gone through
related to each other in a way we never
had before
teased each other
made memories
we bonded in a way we never expected
that's what started it all
-the summer Brooke came home

Maya Serbu

thank you for being the one who danced
in the rain with me
in a crowd of people offering me an
umbrella
-for Kaleigh

you are resilience embodied
The kind of man who looks out for
people, who believes in every side of a
story
Who didn't bat an eye when they started
seeing less,
you became someone in our little town
and i will carry your legacy and last
name with pride
-**Father**

"you're the only thing keeping me sane
sometimes," he laughed.
she stopped and stared at him in wonder
she had never realized that she could
settle the waters of his mind
just like he calmed the storm clouds in
hers
-MK

knowing somebody for your whole life is
easy
being able to trust that person to love
you unconditionally
and to laugh at all your jokes when no
one else does
and to be there to dry your tears at 3am
when you think your world is falling
apart
that is luck
-for Rachel

Maya Serbu

they tease each other like they're 19
they argue like they're 11
they love each other like they're 85
i can't wait to find something like that
-when he met her

Tears of Rose Water

we used to know of each other and play
with the same kids in elementary school
but
now we know each other
we cry, laugh and share secrets
and i don't know how i went so long
without this addition to my life
-for Brooke

Maya Serbu

ever since i met you
i've picked up a lot of your habits
i count the crows on the neighbours'
front lawns
i do things that scare me simply
because, "why not?"
i know the true meaning of loyalty
and i am a firm believer that everything
happens for a reason
-what Kaleigh did to me

you are strength embodied,
the kind of woman who knows her worth,
who doesn't falter if the paycheck does,
who always knows where the "thingy" is
who will do anything for her family
and never let a man second guess her
you are a warrior woman
i hope i inherited your soul
-Mother

our laughter
i can never forget that
it comes in waves
and what makes it so special is that i
only ever laugh that way when i'm with
you
-*the way Abi laughs*

"you always used to look at me like that
when i talked too much," she giggled.
he gave her that same smile he had so
many times before
but this time it made her realize that
soulmates don't always have to be lovers
-like a brother

i can't wait for us to be adult friends
and drink way too much wine
and say we're turning into our mothers
and watch our kids do all the things we
did together
to retell crazy stories,
for all the pain and heartache we went
through to be worth it
and to finally be so genuinely in love
with life
that nothing else can hurt us
-**Our future**

my favourite memories of childhood are
not christmas mornings or summer
vacations
they are the nights of nothingness and
the drives to nowhere
the walks to the gas station for snacks
the long conversations filled of
gibberish
the songs with the lyrics we scream
extra loud
the sleepovers of boy talk and no bras
the laughter that seemed unstoppable
and the days that we wished lasted
forever
-the times of my life

i am from a small town
the neighbours know each other,
the dim street lights tell the kids at
the park "time to go home."
timmy's is the designated meeting spot
the shore is all around you
and everyone says "i can't wait to get
out of here."
i am from a small town
but on the other side of the town
there is a bridge
and city lights
there is hope to be something more,
and that's what i'm going to do.
right here, in this little old town.
-home grown

i live to do what i love
i wake up to write poetry and perform on
stage
to sing more than i speak
that is my oxygen
that is my source of happiness
that is the very meaning of my soul
-Passion

My curves have travelled with me, into
dresses that seemed too tight
stretch marks and cellulite have
tattooed my body, as proof that i have
grown
i've been laughed at by society
for the standards i couldn't meet
but now, looking in the mirror, i see
beauty and strength
glowing brightly enough to outshine
foolish expectations
my stomach isn't flat and yes, my thighs
touch
that is beautiful
so to everyone who is learning to love
themselves, remember:
the size of your heart means more than
the size of your waist, your worth is
determined by how kind your soul is, not
by numbers on a scale
& i wish it didn't take so long to
realize
-*Self Love*

Tears of Rose Water

I have to thank you again,
Your seed was that of a dandelion-
one push and millions of ideas were
planted all around me, encouraging me to
write honestly, damn the system, and put
a line through life's ~~normalities~~.
Without your belief in me,
All of this would have been nothing more
than tangled words in a busy mind.
You did this.
-Nagle

This is for you, yes you. Thank you for
being a seed to grow my dreams. Thank
you for letting me take the poems
planted in my mind and open up my garden
to you.
Thank you for feeling with me, the good
and bad. Because without both storm
clouds and sunlight, seeds would never
bloom.
I hope you've all begun to sprout.
Until next time,
keep growing
changing
accept the storms
appreciate the sunlight
and allow yourself to fearlessly,
Blossom
-For the Readers

Tears of Rose Water

tears of passion
water the roses
with the toughest thorns

www.ingramcontent.com/pod-product-compliance
Lightning Source LLC
Chambersburg PA
CBHW071858020426
42331CB00010B/2566